The Angry Mountain

Claudette Megan Adams

© Copyright text Claudette Megan Adams 1999
© Copyright illustrations Macmillan Education Ltd 1999

All rights reserved. No reproduction, copy or transmission of this publication may be made without written permission.

No paragraph of this publication may be reproduced, copied or transmitted save with written permission or in accordance with the provisions of the Copyright, Designs and Patents Act 1988, or under the terms of any licence permitting limited copying issued by the Copyright Licencing Agency, 90 Tottenham Court Road, London W1P 9HE.

Any person who does any unauthorised act in relation to this publication may be liable to criminal prosecution and civil claims for damages.

First published in 1999 by
MACMILLAN EDUCATION LTD
London and Basingstoke
Companies and representatives throughout the world

ISBN 0-333-74144-7

10 9 8 7 6 5 4 3 2 1
08 07 06 05 04 03 02 01 00 99

This book is printed on paper suitable for recycling and made from fully managed and sustained forest sources.

Printed in Hong Kong

A catalogue record for this book is available from the British Library.

Illustrations by PAT TOURRET / B L Kearley Ltd

Johnny was a little boy who had only one pet, a goat. His father gave it to him when he was five years old. He called it Betsy and they became close friends.

Johnny lived in a little village on a lush, green island. There were plantain and banana trees and brilliant flowers all around. The village felt safe because a big mountain sheltered it from rain and wind that came across the Caribbean Sea.

'Look at the shape of that mountain,' said Johnny's teacher. 'It's a volcano. Long ago fire and burning rocks came out of it and left that great hole at the top. Sometimes a little smoke still comes from the volcano and it rumbles gently. But we believe it's safe.'

'It's like a snoring dragon,' Johnny remarked.

The class laughed.

Johnny's parents were shopkeepers and in the evenings everyone came to their shop. They talked and talked about the day's happenings.

Those were happy times. Johnny used to sit behind the beaded curtain and listen to all the bits of gossip. When he moved, the curtain shook.

'It's like a dancer,' thought Johnny, 'with bells on her toes.' Then his mother sternly sent him to bed.

As he drifted off to sleep, in the room at the back of the shop, Johnny still heard talking and laughter.

Every morning, Johnny went to the pasture and cut some grass for Betsy before he went to school. When he left the goat, Betsy bleated loudly from the pen.
'She wants to come with me,' thought Johnny.

On Saturday mornings, Johnny used to go to the mobile library. Often a friend, Cyril, went with him. As they walked home with their stack of books, they liked to pick mangoes. Sometimes they talked about their afternoon cricket game.

Johnny and his friends played cricket in the middle of a field near the sea. 'Boysie', the school bully, was not very good at cricket and made a fuss when he was out. He did not want to leave the wicket.

Sometimes he said, 'I should have another innings because it's my bat.'

If he did not get his way, Boysie took his bat and ran home. Then their only bats were the flat ends of branches from a coconut tree.

One day the mountain rumbled much louder than usual. There were flames as well as smoke and steam. Johnny's father called to his family, 'Come outside, quickly!'

Hot stones and lava were pouring down the mountainside. The lava was like a stream of yellow and red liquid. It crept down towards the village.

'The dragon's woken up. It's breathing fire!' thought Johnny.

They all hid behind the house and watched. The lava burnt trees and bushes. Ash from the mountain fell everywhere. And some houses caught fire.

'We can't stay here,' said Johnny's father at last. 'Let's take what we can, quickly.'

They loaded a cart and Johnny's father pulled it away from the village. Johnny led the milk cow and Betsy.

'Open the gates, Johnny,' said his father as they went past the fields. 'Let the other cows out. We can't take all of them with us but they can run away from the lava.'

Everyone was hurrying away from the angry volcano. Some people were crying but most were quiet.

The rumbling noises from the mountain got louder and louder. Everyone looked afraid.

'Can it follow us?' Johnny asked. There was a huge cloud in the distance. 'Is it going to catch us?'

'No, we're in a safe area now,' said his father.

But there were no houses in the area. The first night, they slept outside. Then all the families built 'shelters'.

Johnny did not like living in a shelter. 'Our new home is boring,' he thought.

There was no school. But he made a few new friends and they played all day. Mostly they played ring games. Sometimes they read to each other. But they never had a cricket match. There was no space for that sort of game.

At nights, there was no electricity. They all sat outside in the still evening. Only the crickets chirped and the occasional frog croaked. Johnny had his arms round his pet goat. It lay very still.

In the distance the volcano looked beautiful. 'How can something so dangerous be beautiful?' wondered Johnny. 'It looks like a giant Christmas tree in the sky. All lit up with fires — red and yellow.'

They sat there for hours, wondering. The volcano was beautiful but it threatened their lives.

There was always dust in the air. Their eyes smarted. 'I'm not crying,' Johnny told his mother. 'It's the dust.'

His mother was washing clothes. 'The dust is everywhere,' she said. 'As soon as I hang these clothes out they'll be dirty again.'

One day they went back to the village. It was empty and lonely. Thick, grey ash covered everything. A stray dog was roaming around, looking for its owner. Some houses were burnt and had holes in the roofs and walls.

'We can never live here again,' said Johnny's father sadly.

The next evening, his father said, 'We want you to go to England, Johnny. Your uncle and aunt have asked you to stay with them. You'll like that. You'll go by plane and you'll see all sorts of new things.'

'Don't worry, Johnny,' said his mother. 'We'll be safe here and when this is all over, you can come back.'

Very early the next morning, Johnny hugged Betsy for the last time and kissed his parents goodbye. With other children, he had to go to another island to catch a plane. They climbed aboard a boat to take them to the island.

Johnny tried to be brave and told the other children, 'It will be fun on the plane.'

As the boat left the island, the volcano gave a rumble and jets of smoke and steam rose into the air. 'The dragon is angry,' thought Johnny. 'Will it ever leave the island in peace, so that I can return?'

HOP STEP JUMP

HOP

In My Father's Village Michael Palmer 0–333–56866–4
Striped Paint Rosina Umelo 0–333–56865–6
The Slow Chameleon and Shammy's Bride David Cobb 0–333–57728–0
The Walking Talking Flying ABC David Cobb 0–333–56864–8
Raindrops In Africa Margaret House 0–333–58723–5
Sing It, Do It David Cobb 0–333–58721–9
No Problem! Rosina Umelo 0–333–58722–7
Ten Ripe Mangoes David Cobb 0–333–60650–7
The Best Bed In The World Charlotte Mbali 0–333–61584–0
Under The Cotton Tree David Cobb 0–333–61828–9
Lucky Day! Lynn Kramer 0–333–68918–6
The Wake-up Whistler Marianna Brandt 0–333–72414–3
Ask Pungu-Pungu Rita Wooding 0–333–72636–7
Ping Pong P-Pan Barbara Applin 0–333–74142–0

STEP

Choose Me! Lynn Kramer 0–333–56867–2
Nondo The Cow Diane Rasteiro 0–333–57655–1
Sika In The Snow David Cobb 0–333–57672–1
Henry The Last Michael Palmer 0–333–58724–3
My Life On The Wing David Cobb 0–333–58725–1
The Radio Thief Anthony K Johnson 0–333–59514–9
The Grasshopper War Thokozile Chaane 0–333–61411–9
The Numberheads Robyn Roberts 0–333–61412–7
The All-Day Dreamer Karen W Mbugua and Geoff Baier 0–333–61651–0
Honeybrown And The Bees Jill Inyundo 0–333–64191–4
Lissa's Rainbow Dress Joyce Ama Addo 0–333–63310–5
The Bug Collector Gillian Leggat 0–333–63309–1
A Job On The Moon Michael Montgomery 0–333–64330–5
The Lily Pool Jill Inyundo 0–333–67083–3
Want To Be A Strongman? Michael Montgomery 0–333–69877–0
The Cowrie Seekers Shelley Davidow 0–333–68833–3
Ibuka And The Lost Children Sibylla Lewyska 0–333–68834–1
The Angry Mountain Claudette Megan Adams 0–333–74144–7

JUMP

Chichi And The Termites Wendy Ijioma 0–333–57696–9
The Boy Who Ate A Hyena James G D Ngumy 0–333–57694–2
Tickets For The Zed Band Lynn Kramer 0–333–57695–0
Knife Boy Michael Montgomery 0–333–59513–0
Chichi's Nature Diary Wendy Ijioma 0–333–59512–2
Fair Shares Lynn Kramer 0–333–59511–4
Paa Bena And The New Canoe Phyllis Addy 0–333–59857–1
Chimpanzee Rescue Margaret House 0–333–60651–5
The Calabash And The Box Bobson Sesay 0–333–61826–2
Check, Come Here! Edison Yongai 0–333–61827–0
You Can't Grow Footballs From Seeds Margaret Spencer 0–333–62218–9
Pepi Mazamban, Mender of Cars, Age 10 James Mason 0–333–63308–3
Water Girl Michael Montgomery 0–333–64329–1
Two Eggs For The President Marianna Brandt 0–333–66810–3
Search For The Stone Bird Shelley Davidow 0–333–69876–2
Tofu in Trouble Dawn Ridgway 0–333–68200–9
Fisherwoman Effie Adrienne 0–333–74143–9
The Taming Of Pudding Pan Berna McIntosh 0–333–74141–2

POETRY

On The Poetry Bus ed. David Cobb 0–333–64070–5
Sometimes When It Rains Achirri Chi-Bikon 0–333–63307–5
Riding A Rainbow Achirri Chi-Bikom 0–333–67160–0